# THE LITTLE BOOK OF
# HOCKEY SWEATERS
# VOLUME 2

# The Little Book of Hockey Sweaters

## Volume 2

**Andrew Podnieks**

**Illustrated by Anthony Jenkins**

KEY PORTER  BOOKS

# Contents

**DANIEL ALFREDSSON** might become one of the rarest of NHLers: a player who spends his entire career with one team, *and* who wears the same number his entire career. In 1994, the Swede was drafted by Ottawa a lowly 133rd overall and joined the Senators a year later. In his eleven full seasons, "Alfie" has scored more than 700 points for the Senators, and the team has missed the playoffs only once—ironically, in his first season, when he won the Calder Trophy as the National Hockey League's best rookie. In 2006–07, he had a breakout year with 43 goals and 103 points. In 2007–08, he formed one of the most potent threesomes in the league with sniper Dany Heatley and set-up man Jason Spezza, finishing with 89 points. His number has been as consistent as the point-a-game pace he has maintained throughout his career. As he explained, "I had two choices when I picked my number: 22 and 11. Eleven was the number I had when I played soccer, so it was an easy choice." And 11 has been his number ever since.

**IF NOT FOR A CONCUSSION,** the life and career of Jason Allison might have been much grander than it was. He was a first-round draft choice with Washington in 1993, and in 552 regular-season games in the NHL he had 485 points. His best year came in 2000–01, with Boston, when he had 36 goals and 95 points. The next year, he signed with Los Angeles and slumped a bit, and then, early the following season, he suffered a concussion and missed two and a half years. In 2005, feeling healthy again, he made one last attempt to salvage his career, but the 2005–06 season with Toronto wasn't as successful as he had hoped, even though he managed 17 goals. At every stop in his career, 41 was his number of choice. The number was unavailable for a brief period in Boston, so he simply reversed the digits and went with 14. As he explained, "When I got to my junior team [the London Knights of the Ontario Hockey League], there were only a couple of rookies and all the numbers between 1 and 39 were pretty much gone. So, I took 41 and stuck with it." It stood him in good stead for more than a decade, and Allison retired after a fine, though injury-shortened, career.

**DRAFTED TENTH OVERALL IN 1998,** Nik Antropov was a tall, gangly forward with loads of potential and an uncanny ability to suffer injuries. In his first eight seasons with Toronto, Antropov averaged just 53 games and never scored more than 18 goals, but in 2007–08 he had a career year with 26. Antropov's numeric history with his one and only NHL team has been all over the map, as inconsistent as his on-ice performance has been. As a teenager in Kazakhstan, he always wore number 19, but when Antropov joined the Leafs to start the 1999–2000 season, that number belonged to Freddy Modin, so he went with 9 instead. After a couple of seasons, he decided the number didn't agree with him, so he requested 11, which was his number with Moscow Dynamo in 1998–99. Then the Leafs acquired Owen Nolan, a longtime user of 11, in a trade with San Jose, so Antropov acquiesced and switched to 80, the year of his birth. He has used it for several years now, and has had enough success with it that he isn't likely to change—for a while, anyway.

**SEAN AVERY HAS BECOME** so well known as a super-pest that it's easy to forget how humbly his NHL career began. After playing his junior hockey with Owen Sound and Kingston of the OHL, Avery was not drafted by any NHL team. The Detroit Red Wings, however, must have seen something in him that no one else did because they signed him as a free agent in 1999 and put him in their farm system. Avery made it to Detroit for parts of 2001–02 and 2002–03; with no seniority or leverage, he wore the unspectacular number 42. But when the Wings traded him to Los Angeles in March 2003, he received 19, the number he always wore when given the opportunity. This was in honour of his hero, Steve Yzerman, the long-time Detroit captain, who of course had 19 when Avery first got to Detroit. Avery wore 19 for the better part of three years in L.A., but when he was traded to the Rangers he had to choose another number because Blair Betts had 19. Avery decided to flip the 9 and make it a 6, ending up with 16. At the end of the 2006–07 season, Betts himself was the victim of a numeric power play. The team signed Scott Gomez and Chris Drury in the off-season, and Gomez wanted 19, forcing Betts also to switch. Avery has kept 16, but fans can be sure that if he ever goes to a team where 19 is available, he'll take it.

**WADE BELAK** had an amazingly long run with the Toronto Maple Leafs before being sent to Florida in a deadline deal in February 2008. For parts of eight seasons, he was an Everyman who played both as a defenceman and a winger, renowned primarily as a tough guy who protected the team's more skilled players and got physical when the game required it. He might not see a lot of ice time, but his mere presence on the bench can cause opposing coaches to reconsider their game plan. Belak's NHL career began in Colorado, where he played only a few games over three seasons before a trade midway through the 1998–99 season sent him to Calgary. Two years later, in February 2001, he was claimed off waivers by the Leafs. Belak wore number 6 in Colorado and had two numbers in Calgary, 29 and 4. When he got to the Leafs he took 2, but as soon as he had the chance, he switched to 3 in honour of Dave Manson. As Belak explained, "He [Manson] wore number 3 when he was a Leaf and he was one of my boyhood idols." The Panthers already had a number 3 in Karlis Skrastins, so Belak has lately been seen in number 33.

**THE ONCE-BRIGHT CAREER** of Todd Bertuzzi would be all but over if not for the blind devotion of Anaheim general manager Brian Burke. Bertuzzi has been a controversial figure since he attacked Steve Moore on March 8, 2004, after which he was suspended indefinitely. After he was reinstated in August 2005, the Vancouver Canucks traded him to Florida, but that stint was marred by a back injury and he managed to score just one goal in seven games. The Panthers sent Bertuzzi to Detroit for a junior prospect, Shawn Matthias, and a couple of draft choices, but Burke—who had been the GM in Vancouver when "Big Bert" played there—rescued him by signing him as a free agent in 2007. At his best, Bertuzzi was a power forward, and his best season was as a Canuck in 2002–03, when he scored 46 goals and 97 points. Bertuzzi began his career with the Islanders, wearing his preferred number, 44. When he got to Vancouver, he had to settle for 27 briefly before getting 44, which he also wore in both Florida and Detroit. With the Ducks, however, the number belonged to the popular Rob Niedermayer. Bertuzzi did the opposite of what many players do: instead of doubling a favourite number, he "singled" his and chose the simple 4—an uncommon number for a forward, but one that was consistent with his desire to wear a number with a 4 in it.

**TOM BLADON WAS DRAFTED** 23rd overall by
Philadelphia in the 1972 Amateur Draft, which is why
he wore 23 when he started with the Flyers that very fall.
His teammate, Bill Barber, was selected seventh in the
same draft, and that's why Barber wore 7. The difference
was that Barber stayed with the Flyers his whole career
and wore only that number, while Bladon moved around
and changed numbers. In fact, he also wore numbers 3
and 4 with the Flyers during his six years with the team,
and in Pittsburgh he wore number 2 for two seasons
(1978–80). Bladon returned to 23 for a year in Edmonton,
but later took 21 in Winnipeg and 4 in Detroit. The fact
that he and Barber wore their draft selections on the
backs of their sweaters, while a bit gimmicky, actually
made them numeric pioneers.

**COMING OFF A 40-GOAL SEASON** with the New York Islanders in 2006–07, Jason Blake looked like a potential scoring superstar who had been flying under the radar by playing in a less-celebrated hockey market (Long Island). When the Leafs signed him in the summer of 2007, there were high hopes that his offensive heroics would continue in one of hockey's capitals. Alas, it was not to be. Soon after the start of the season, Blake was diagnosed with chronic myelogenous leukemia, a treatable form of cancer of the blood cells. He continued to play every night, and was among the league leaders in shots on goal, but he couldn't find the back of the net for all the world. Halfway through the season, he had only 6 goals, and although he appeared in all 82 games, he ended up with just 15 goals. Blake began his career in Los Angeles in 1998–99, wearing number 11, but his number of choice had always been 5, which he had used during his three-year career at the University of North Dakota. When he was traded to the Islanders in early 2001, he couldn't wear 5 because that number was hanging from the rafters in honour of Hall of Fame defenceman Denis Potvin, so Blake asked his daughter, Lauren, what she thought of 55 instead. She liked it, and Blake adopted it as his new number. He kept it with the Leafs, a team that had also retired number 5 (for Bill Barilko).

BLAKE

55

55?

**AS A KID GROWING UP** in Simcoe, Ontario, Rob Blake always idolized Montreal great Larry Robinson. "Big Bird" played with the Canadiens most of his career, winning six Stanley Cups and being inducted into the Hockey Hall of Fame as soon as he became eligible. His number, 19, hangs from the rafters of the Bell Centre in Montreal. Blake went on to become a star defenceman in his own right. He was drafted by Los Angeles in 1988, while he was attending Bowling Green State University, and he was called up to play his first NHL game with the Kings on March 27, 1990. Of course, he wanted to wear number 19, but there was one problem: the player who already had that number was none other than Larry Robinson himself! Robinson closed out his career with a three-year run with the Kings (1989–92) after the Canadiens thought his playing days were over. As a result, Blake was assigned number 4, but got to play with his idol for three seasons. Traded to Colorado in 2001, he rejoined the Kings as a free agent, and as team captain, in 2007–08. He is a rare example of a player who has worn the same number in every NHL game he has ever played—1,127 and counting.

**DEFENCEMAN DAN BOYLE'S STORY** is an inspiring one. The native of Ottawa, Ontario, played hockey at Miami University (in Oxford, Ohio—go figure), but during his four years with the Red Hawks (1994–98), he made little impression on NHL scouts. The drafts came and went, and no team selected Boyle. At the end of his senior year, though, the Florida Panthers signed him as a free agent. Boyle spent most of the next two seasons in the minors, finally earning a permanent spot in the NHL in 2000. In January 2002, however, he was traded to Tampa Bay for nothing more than a fifth-round draft choice. Boyle has been with the Lightning ever since. As a call-up in Florida, he wore numbers 26 and 6, and when he got to Tampa he initially had to settle for 29. He soon got into the number 22 sweater that he had always wanted, and he has worn it ever since. Why 22? That's the number of his idol, Rick Tocchet, a power forward. Boyle, a different kind of player at a different position, has nonetheless displayed a level of skill and class while wearing the sweater that would make its original wearer, Tocchet, proud.

**ALTHOUGH HARDLY A SUPERSTAR**, hard-working Chris Campoli has established himself as a reliable defenceman with the New York Islanders since making the team out of training camp in September 2005. He was drafted a lowly 227th overall by the team in 2004, but, undaunted, he pursued his NHL dream with a single-minded conviction that belied his draft position. As a bonus, the Toronto native has been able to wear number 14 from the start of his still brief career, a number with great significance for him. His father, Gino, had played baseball with a senior team that won the Ontario provincial championship in 1982. Gino was a catcher, and wore number 14 his entire career.

**SOMETIMES A PLAYER** doesn't care much about a particular number until he gets it and then finds meaning in it. Such is the case with Keith Carney, who has worn number 3 since 1997. In a career that has spanned seventeen seasons and more than a thousand games with six different NHL teams, the big defenceman has been nothing if not a survivor. Early in his career with Buffalo, Carney wore 6 and 26 before getting number 4, which he kept when he became a Chicago Blackhawk. None held any particular significance. When he was traded to Phoenix midway through the 1997–98 season, he was given number 3 and again thought nothing of it. Then, his wife, Amy, gave birth to triplets, all boys—Aidan, Cole, and Kade—and *voilà!* The number 3 had a meaning. Carney has been able to keep the number in stops with Vancouver and, more recently, Minnesota. And so a number that he once wore as a mere after-thought has come to mean the world to him, a constant reminder of his family.

**AS A TEEN,** Anson Carter wasn't considered much of an NHL prospect, and the Quebec Nordiques drafted him way down at 220th overall in 1992. But Carter was a late bloomer, and in four years at Michigan State University he developed into a proven scorer as well as a physical player. He was traded to Washington before he ever played in an NHL game, though, and then was sent to Boston after only 19 games. Carter had three good years with the Bruins, but his career subsequently found him changing teams—and crossing the continent—frequently. Seven more teams—Edmonton, the Rangers, Washington, Los Angeles, Vancouver, Columbus, and, finally, Carolina—took turns trying to get Carter to produce the way they felt he could. Carter's most famous moment came with Team Canada in the gold-medal game of the 2003 World Championship, when he scored in dramatic fashion in overtime to clinch a 3–2 victory over Sweden. Carter's numeric history was far more consistent. As a kid, he was a Mike Bossy fan, so he sought out number 22 whenever he could get it. At his first NHL stop, in Washington, the number was taken by Steve Konowalchuk, so Carter stayed with the idea of double digits, bumping himself up to 33. The pattern repeated in Boston, where he was 11 and 33; in Edmonton, New York, and Washington he was able to wear 22; with the Kings, he had to revert to 11. His last three NHL stops—Vancouver, Columbus, and Carolina—all saw Carter go with double 7s. In 2007, he left to play in Europe, the promise of his career unfulfilled save the gold medal glory.

**IF NOT FOR BOBBY ORR,** it might reasonably be argued that Paul Coffey was the greatest defenceman the game has ever known. A poetically brilliant skater, a passer with pinpoint accuracy, and an offensive threat that made him the equal of a fourth forward on every shift, Coffey retired in 2001 with 1,531 regular-season points, a record for defencemen at the time. During his illustrious twenty-one-year career, he wore only three numbers, two of which were clearly connected. The third was also special to Coffey, though the reason wasn't as obvious. Coffey started with the great Edmonton Oilers in 1980, and over the next seven years he helped the team win four Stanley Cups, always wearing number 7. But in the summer of 1987 he ran into contract troubles with the team's coach and general manager, Glen Sather, and was traded to Pittsburgh, where Rod Buskas was the incumbent number 7. Coffey doubled the digit and went with 77, the number he then wore for a series of teams—Los Angeles, Detroit, Hartford, Philadelphia, Chicago, and Carolina. He ended his career with Boston in 2000–01, playing 18 games with the Bruins. That was the one place where 77 was unavailable, as Ray Bourque was wearing it. So Coffey went with an unusual alternative: 74, so chosen because he wore 7 with the Oilers and won four Stanley Cups with the team.

**PINT-SIZED MIKE COMRIE** was as popular a player as they come in Edmonton when he joined the Oilers to start the 2000–01 season. He was born in Edmonton, played provincial junior hockey in nearby St. Albert, and was an inspiration both because he was a lower draft choice (91st overall in 1999) and was a small guy who played with skill. Indeed, after scoring 8 goals in half a season as a rookie, he exploded with 33 the following year, many of them the result of great rushes, fancy dekes, and entertaining moves around the net. Despite the fact that Comrie slumped to just 20 goals the year after, he started to demand a larger contract, which didn't endear him to management. The result was a trade to Philadelphia, and Comrie has been a restless soul ever since. In 2003–04, he lasted only 21 games (scoring just four times) with the Flyers before they sent him to Phoenix, where he had only 8 goals in 28 games. After the year lost to the lockout (2004–05), Comrie had an excellent season (30 goals), but soon was on the move to Ottawa and, most recently, the New York Islanders. At every stop and for every game, Comrie has been able to wear number 89, the number he was assigned at his first training camp.

**IT WASN'T A DIFFICULT DECISION** for Pete Conacher. In fact, it wasn't a decision he made at all. While the name Conacher resonates with greatness for any NHL fan, the name Pete indicates the least accomplished of the family. There was his father, Charlie, one of the greatest players in Toronto Maple Leafs history, and an uncle, Roy, another Hall of Famer who won the Stanley Cup with Boston in 1939 and 1941, went off to war, and returned to resume his NHL career. Another uncle, Lionel, was also considered one of the greatest players of the NHL's early years. But Pete didn't have the same skills. He wasn't flashy, wasn't a top scorer, like his dad and uncles. When the woeful Chicago Black Hawks called him up from the farm in St. Louis, their decision was as much a marketing ploy as it was a sign of genuine belief in his talent. After all, any Conacher arriving in the NHL in 1952 was big news. Of course, the Hawks gave him number 9, the same number as Charlie and Roy, and Pete dutifully wore it, even though he bore no on-ice resemblance. Still, it made for a great story, and it gave Pete the chance to join his relatives as members of the elite league.

**WHEN THE NEW YORK RANGERS** signed both Chris Drury and Scott Gomez as free agents in the summer of 2007, they managed to acquire two of the few marquee names available. But what team president Glen Sather didn't realize right away was that he had set a major numbers game in motion, because both Gomez and Drury had worn 23 for their respective teams (Drury with Buffalo and Gomez with New Jersey). What to do? When the two were introduced to the media, they were each given new sweaters with the number 23 on the back, but of course this arrangement wouldn't work in the long run. So, Sather simply flipped a puck. Drury won the toss and kept number 23, while Gomez opted for 19. Drury wears 23 in honour of his hero, the New York Yankees star Don Mattingly. Gomez, on the other hand, was assigned 23 when he started his NHL career with the Devils, having worn 19 and 11 in university. Since the Rangers had retired number 11, worn by Mark Messier, Gomez opted for 19—a number that belonged to Blair Betts. Gomez negotiated a deal whereby he could get number 19 by donating $10,000 to the Rangers' Garden of Dreams Foundation in Betts's name, a worthy deal if ever there was one. In the end, both Drury and Gomez were happy, and charity benefited as well.

**ANDERS ERIKSSON** has really racked up the frequent-flier miles during his career. The Swedish defenceman, who started out at home with MoDo in 1993, hasn't stayed in any one place for long. Detroit drafted him 22nd overall in 1993, and Eriksson attended the Red Wings' training camp two years later. He was assigned to their Adirondack farm team and was called up for one game, and in 1996–97 he played twenty-three times with Detroit. The next year, Eriksson found full-time work with the parent club and was part of the Wings' Stanley Cup triumph in the spring of 1998, but he was traded to the lowly Chicago Blackhawks late in 1998–99. From Chicago he moved on to Florida, Toronto, and Columbus, and he seemed destined to be one of those bubble players for whom the lockout spelled the end. Eriksson returned to Sweden for 2004–05 and moved on to Russia for part of the next year, but he was not yet done in North America. The Blue Jackets re-signed him, and in 2007–08 he went to Calgary, where he played the full season. Although he has worn a plethora of numbers during his career, Eriksson is partial to the number 2, which he used with Columbus for two years as a tribute to the great defenceman Slava Fetisov. Eriksson will never be confused for the iconic Russian, but the connection, for Eriksson, exists, if only numerically.

**ARGUABLY HOCKEY'S FIRST GOON**—or designated fighter—John Ferguson played his entire, brief career (1963–71) with Montreal. Although he was famous for his fists, he was hardly a bench warmer during Montreal's "silent dynasty" of the 1960s (a decade in which the Canadiens won four Stanley Cups, a feat overshadowed by the Toronto Maple Leafs, who won an equal number of Cups in the same span). Ferguson was on five Stanley Cup–winning teams in his eight seasons. He had 1,214 penalties in minutes over 500 regular-season games, and another 260 minutes in 85 playoff games. Nonetheless, he also averaged 18 goals a year, peaking in 1968–69 with 29 goals and 185 PIM. Ferguson was given his famous number 22 at training camp, and his affection for the number grew to the point that it became an extension of his personality. A lover of horses, he ran a farm called Two-Two Stables, and his car's licence plate number was a simple 22.

**THOUGH HE'S NOT A HOUSEHOLD NAME** in North America, Petr Fical has been one of Germany's steadiest players and a frequent member of the national team. Born in the Czech Republic, the right winger played junior hockey in his homeland, and when he wasn't drafted by a National Hockey League team he graduated to the Deutsche Eishockey-Liga, the premier league in Germany. Whenever possible, Fical wears number 27. He has played at four major tournaments—the 2004 World Cup, the 2005 and 2007 World Championships, and the 2006 Olympics in Turin—and on each occasion his favourite number has been unavailable, so he has had to flip the digits and wear 72. The original 27 is important to him because it is the date of his father's birthday. It remains his number in league play, but he has worn 72 so consistently in international play that he now considers it his "national" number.

**MIKE FISHER HAS A STORY** for every number he has selected—and there have been a few. The most straight-forward tale involves his NHL number, 12, which he has worn in every game he's played, all of them with Ottawa, starting in 1999. Drafted 44th overall by the Senators in 1998, Fisher's number since childhood had been 7. When he attended his first Ottawa training camp in the fall of 1999, though, 7 was taken by Rob Zamuner, so Fisher was assigned 12. When Fisher made the team he saw no reason to change. At the end of the 2004–05 season, he was invited to play for Canada at the World Championship in Austria. He accepted, but he couldn't wear 12 because it was reserved by Hockey Canada for the Calgary Flames star Jarome Iginla. To make matters worse, Fisher couldn't even wear 7 because it had been claimed by Vancouver's Brendan Morrison, who had seniority. So, Fisher went with 17 because it had the 1 from Ottawa and the 7 from childhood. During the 2004–05 lockout, when Fisher spent the year playing for Zug in the Swiss league, he was able to nab number 7. It might not be simple, but it all makes sense.

**LIKE MANY PLAYERS,** Ftorek wore a number to emulate a hero, but his story is richer than that. As a boy growing up in Needham, Massachusetts, just outside of Boston, Ftorek was a big fan of the Bruins' Fleming Mackell. He was able to meet the star once as a boy, and an indelible image remained. "He brought me into the Bruins' dressing room," Ftorek explained, "cut down a stick to my size, and took me around to shake hands with all the Bruins. He left an image in my mind that was very nice, and that's why I've always worn number 8." Well, not always. When he joined Detroit for part of the 1972–73 season, Guy Charron had 8, so Ftorek went with 23. The next year, Ftorek took 15 when called up from the minors, but in 1974 he jumped to the World Hockey Association, where the Phoenix Roadrunners were just getting started, and he was able to score his prized number 8. When the Roadrunners folded a few years later, he caught on with the Cincinnati Stingers, who already had a number 8, Claude Larose. Larose was the team's top player, while Ftorek had been named the WHA's most valuable player in 1976–77. The team couldn't see a way to resolve the dilemma, so it petitioned the league to allow both players to wear number 8. Incredibly, the league agreed!

**Rod Gilbert**

**HALL OF FAMER ROD GILBERT** played in an era when players often remained with one team for their entire careers. In his case, it was the New York Rangers, the team he joined as a nineteen-year-old in 1960, and the team he retired from eighteen years and 1,065 regular-season games later. Gilbert played his junior hockey with the legendary Guelph Biltmores of the Ontario Hockey Association, during which time he wore number 9 in honour of his hero, Andy Bathgate of the Rangers. When Gilbert made the team in 1960, he couldn't wear 9 because Bathgate was still a Rangers forward, so he accepted number 16. Bathgate was traded to the Leafs during the 1963–64 season, but Gilbert didn't have the nerve to claim the now-vacant 9. Instead, he went for number 7 because, he says, "Playing in New York, I became a Yankees fan, and I admired Mickey Mantle." Gilbert wore 7 the rest of his playing days.

**ALTHOUGH NO PLAYER** in the history of the game has
won more Stanley Cups than Henri Richard (eleven), he
is always considered the second-best player in his family. Top
marks always go to older brother Maurice, the Rocket,
who may not have had as lengthy a career or even
scored as many points, but whose play was far more
electrifying and whose scoring exploits were the stuff of
history and myth. Enter young Michel Goulet, a Quebecker
who idolized the Rocket. He always wanted to wear
Maurice's number 9, and for one year, 1978–79, he was
able to do so, with the Birmingham Bulls of the WHA.
A year later, when the WHA and NHL merged, Goulet
happily found himself playing for the Quebec Nordiques.
The number 9, however, was already assigned to Real
Cloutier, so Goulet remembered the second-best
member of the Richard family and took Henri's number,
16. He wore that number for every NHL game he played
in, through eleven years with the Nordiques and five
more with Chicago, some 1,089 games in all. Henri
would have been honoured, but maybe more so if 16
had been Goulet's first choice, rather than his second.

**OVER A PERIPATETIC CAREER** that spanned nearly two decades and many, many teams, Greg Hawgood was a survivor. A low draft choice by Boston in 1986, he made his NHL debut with the Bruins three years later. Although he played some twelve seasons in the big league, he got into only 474 games between long stretches in the minors. As a Kamloops Blazer, Hawgood had worn number 4, in honour of his hero, Bobby Orr. Of course, during his big-league career no one could possibly confuse him for even a pale imitation of the great Orr. With each of the eight NHL teams Hawgood played for, something invariably came up that prevented him from getting number 4. In Boston, it hung from the rafters, retired in honour of Orr. (Oddly enough, number 4 is retired in Kamloops— to honour Hawgood!) Consequently, Hawgood wore many unusual numbers—35, 38, 39—as a Bruin before settling on 40, as close to 4 as he could get. In Edmonton, Kevin Lowe had the number, in Philadelphia, it was retired for the late Barry Ashbee, and in Florida it was used by Kevin Brown. Finally, after a late-season trade to Pittsburgh in 1994, Hawgood was able to wear number 4 over a long stretch, with the Penguins, San Jose, and Vancouver. But his last NHL stop was in Dallas (2001–02), where Dave Manson wore number 4, so Hawgood ended his career in a number 28 sweater—a long way from Orr, to be sure.

**HE HAS BEEN** among the NHL's top goal scorers over the last few years, but for Dany Heatley the going has been rough away from the rink. He joined Atlanta in 2001 after the Thrashers selected him second overall. But his career was marred by an incident during training camp in September 2003. He was driving a car that crashed into a fence, and his teammate and passenger, Dan Snyder, went into a coma. A few days later he was taken off life support and passed away. Meanwhile, Heatley missed half the season recovering from his own injuries. In a remarkable display of forgiveness, the Snyder family pleaded with the courts not to impose a jail sentence on Heatley, but Heatley had a tough time recovering from the emotional scars left by the car crash. Shortly before the start of the 2005–06 season, he was traded to Ottawa, and the change of venue gave him a fresh start. He scored 50 goals in both that season and the next, and he developed into one of the best players in the league. Heatley always wore 15 with Atlanta, but when he was introduced to Ottawa he sported a 51 sweater because Peter Schaefer was the incumbent 15. Quipped Heatley about the awkward 51, "I haven't had a chance to negotiate with him [Schaefer] yet." No need. The next day, Heatley was on the receiving end of another kind gesture as Schaefer offered him 15 and switched to 27.

*Dany Heatley*

**AN UNSPECTACULAR** but valuable utility forward, Dan Hinote was drafted well down the list of available talent in 1996, at 167th overall by the Colorado Avalanche, the most recent winners of the Stanley Cup. Hinote was no overnight success—he split the next three years and part of a fourth between the junior Oshawa Generals and the Avs' AHL affiliate, the Hershey Bears. But once he was called up, he made the most of his chance and has remained in the big league. At first, he took the number he was given, 38, but when he had the chance, he switched immediately to 13, his dad's lucky number. Hinote retained 13 for the rest of his years with Colorado, but when he signed as a free agent with St. Louis in the summer of 2006, he had to change numbers because Bill Guerin already had 13. He settled for 58, a number whose digits add up to 13. A year later, when Guerin signed with the Islanders, Hinote immediately snapped up 13, making his dad proud and happy once again.

**TOMAS HOLMSTROM WASN'T EVEN DRAFTED** by an NHL team until he was twenty-one years old, and even then Detroit didn't select him until 257th overall in 1994—indicating low expectations, indeed. Despite his rather advanced draft age, Holmstrom's NHL debut was delayed even further. The Red Wings wanted him to keep playing in Sweden, with Lulea, and it wasn't until 1996, when he was twenty-four, that he finally cracked the Red Wings lineup. His timing was impeccable. Even though he played a minor role during that 1996–97 season, he was part of a Cup-winning team. He later won two more championships in Detroit, playing an ever more prominent role, and in 2006–07 he scored 30 goals, an impressive benchmark in an era of low-scoring hockey. Holmstrom wore number 15 his first season, but in the summer of 1997 the Red Wings signed Dmitri Mironov, a longtime wearer of that number. Holmstrom gave up the number to the senior Mironov and chose 96 instead, as a reminder of the year he made the NHL. Holmstrom has worn it ever since, and his career, now eleven years old, has seen him play every game with the same team, a rarity in the modern game.

**BECAUSE NHL TALENT** is spread so thinly over thirty teams, the name Nathan Horton might not stand out or leave a great impression at first, but make no mistake, Horton is one of the more skilled players in the game. He was drafted third overall by Florida in 2003, behind only Marc-Andre Fleury and Eric Staal, and he has quickly developed into a star player. As a rookie, he scored 14 goals, but in his second and third years he had 28 and 31 goals, respectively, proving his worth as an offensive talent on a team in desperate need of scoring. When he got to the Panthers, Horton originally wanted to wear number 10, but when he found out the last player with that number was Pavel Bure, he demurred and opted for 16. "A little less pressure," Horton explained with a smile about the changed digits. Unfortunately, this explanation was given to a group of reporters among whom was Randy Moller, a former player and, coincidentally, the last wearer of 16 with the Panthers! Taking it all in stride, Moller joked, "I'm still distraught the Panthers never retired that number." They might just raise it to the rafters one day, but chances are that if they do the nameplate will read "Horton," not "Moller."

**NUMERICALLY SPEAKING,** Rejean Houle's happiest days were in the WHA when he played for the Quebec Nordiques (1973–76). Houle had started his NHL career with the Montreal Canadiens in 1969, but the lure of a big-money contract was too good to resist and he left the NHL for the upstart league. It was with the Nordiques that he was able to wear number 5, his preferred number because of his boyhood idol, the great Bernie "Boom Boom" Geoffrion. But when Houle first got to the Habs, he was a rookie call-up who had no influence with the trainer, who handed him number 11. Later, defenceman Guy Lapointe had number 5, so Houle was given 14 for no particular reason. After three years in the WHA, Houle returned to the Canadiens and, since Lapointe was still with the team, selected number 15, because at least it had a 5 in it. And so, for the last seven years of his pro career, Houle became known as a 15, even though in his heart of hearts he was partial to Boom Boom's 5.

## Bobby Hull

**BY THE TIME HE RETIRED IN 1980,** Bobby Hull was the highest-scoring left winger in NHL history and a player who had earned enormous respect for his off-ice actions as well. It was his signing by the Winnipeg Jets, in the summer of 1972, that allowed many players to earn millions of dollars they wouldn't have been paid in the closed world of the NHL. When Hull first joined the Chicago Black Hawks as a rookie for the 1957–58 season, he was skating in a six-team league and clubs travelled everywhere by train. This was important because, when he was assigned the number 16, it meant he was relegated to an upper berth in sleeper cars on road trips. Veterans with lower sweater numbers always got the far more comfortable lower berths. When Hull had developed into a true star, he was offered the number 7 and took it immediately—not because of an association with an idol so much as the promise of a lower berth and sounder sleep! But Hull never really wanted 7, so when the chance came to switch again, to the more prestigious 9, he grabbed it. "I've been wanting number 9 for about five years now," he admitted after the change. "Tod Sloan had it at the time. I guess it was because of [Gordie] Howe wearing the number." Ironically, Hull's final games took place with the Hartford Whalers, where Howe was still playing. Hull had to change numbers and opted for 16, a nostalgic nod to his first games as a pro.

**FORWARD LARRY JEFFREY** had a solid NHL career that carried him through the 1960s. He made his debut with the Detroit Red Wings in 1961–62, and later played with the Leafs during their Cup run in 1966–67. After expansion, he finished his career with a third Original Six team, the Rangers, for whom he played two seasons (1967–69). For most of his first two seasons he was able to get the number he really wanted, number 21, which was taken by more senior players in Toronto and New York (Bobby Baun and Camille Henry, respectively). The number 21 held particular significance for him. You see, Jeffrey was born in Goderich, Ontario, and his house was located on Highway 21!

**THE LOS ANGELES KINGS** expected big things from Olli Jokinen when they drafted him third overall in the 1997 Entry Draft, but after only 74 games over two years, before he could deliver on those expectations, they traded him to the New York Islanders. Had they been more patient, the Kings would have been rewarded. As the Islanders would have been, except they also traded him, to Florida, after just one season, during which Jokinen scored only 11 goals. In Florida, he was given great support from coach Mike Keenan, and soon the Finn was named captain. Jokinen responded and has averaged more than 30 goals a year over the last five seasons—all-star numbers, to be sure. Jokinen had always worn number 12, but when he got to the Kings during the 1997–98 season, Roman Vopat had the number. Jokinen reversed the digits and went with 21, and changed to 12 a year later when he played the full season with the team (Vopat was in the minors most of 1998–99, thus relinquishing his claim on the number). When Jokinen got to the Islanders, Mike Watt had 12, so Jokinen took 62, because at least there was a 2 in the number. When he moved on to Florida in September 2000, number 12 was again available and has been his number since. During the 2004–05 lockout, Jokinen returned to Finland for part of the season and wore 84, since 8 plus 4 equals 12.

**TORONTO MAPLE LEAFS** defenceman Tomas Kaberle is one of the great success stories of the NHL's Entry Draft. Selected a lowly 204th overall in 1996, he has become the team's most consistent and reliable blueliner. Durable and disciplined, he has missed only a few games to injury and is one of the least penalized players in the league. Kaberle took two years to develop before making the Leafs at training camp in 1998, but his success is not unique within his family. Brother Frantisek is also an NHLer, and their father, Frantisek Sr., was a highly successful player in the former Czechoslovakia, both at the national and international levels. Indeed, Frantisek Sr., played in five World Championships in the 1970s as well as at the 1980 Olympics. Tomas always wore number 12 as a kid, but when he made the Leafs that number belonged to Kris King. Tomas opted instead for 15, his father's number. It has been his only NHL number, and the Leafs have been his only NHL team.

Only Team

Only number

**LIKE HIS OLDER BROTHER PAUL**, Steve Kariya played hockey at the University of Maine as a means to launch his NHL career, but unlike his brother, Steve wasn't attracting huge attention from NHL scouts after four years with the Black Bears. Often the skill of an older brother leads to scouting reports that suggest "the younger brother is even better," but no such reports circulated about Steve. Skilled as he was, he was much smaller than Paul, who was already considered one of the league's smaller players. Because of his last name, the Vancouver Canucks gave Steve three years to develop, but he was unable to do so. As a pro rookie in 1999–2000, he played part of the year in the AHL and also got into 45 games for the Canucks, although he only managed 8 goals and 19 points, not huge numbers. The next year, however, Steve started the season with Vancouver, but, after scoring only once in 17 games, he was demoted. The year after, he earned even less NHL time—three games in all. Kariya took the hint and signed with Ilves Tampere in Finland in 2004 and has had a very successful European career ever since. But when he was with Vancouver, he wore number 18 because he always said he'd be twice as good as his brother (Paul has usually worn number 9). It wasn't true, but the kid had plenty of gumption to feel that way all the same.

**THE BOSTON BRUINS** feel they have a superstar in the making in Phil Kessel. They drafted him fifth overall in 2006, and he surprised even the coaching staff by making the team in his first training camp that fall. Kessel was no ordinary eighteen-year-old, however. He spent two important years with the innovative U.S. National Team Development Program in Ann Arbor, Michigan, a program run by USA Hockey that focuses on a small group of the most talented teenagers in the country. It was after only two years with the program that he went to the University of Minnesota, and a year later he was in the NHL. Although he wears 81 with the Bruins, Kessel still has a few sticks with the number 26 on them. That's because when he first came to the Bruins, he was still using his sticks from U of M, where he wore 26. Number 8 is his number of choice, however, and that's what he wore for Team USA at the 2007 World Championship in Moscow. But he couldn't have that number with the Bruins because it hangs in the rafters to honour Cam Neely. Kessel instead went with 81, not because of any proximity to 8 but because that was the number he was issued his first year with the National Team Development Program. "All the first-year guys had to take high numbers," he explained.

**UNTIL HE FOUND A HOME IN TORONTO,** Chad Kilger was something of a vagabond fourth-liner in the NHL, never staying in one city for any length of time. Amazingly, he was drafted fourth overall by Anaheim in 1995, but he has not lived up to the expectations of such a high selection. Nonetheless, he has played in the league for more than a decade. He began with the Ducks in 1995–96, but they traded him to Winnipeg halfway through the year. That summer, the team moved to Phoenix, and he moved with them, but he played only a few games over the next two seasons, spending most of his time in the minors. Stops in Chicago and Edmonton were next, before he settled in Montreal, where he was a utility player for three years. But the Canadiens put him on waivers in March 2004, and it was then that the Leafs claimed him. Kilger always went for number 18 whenever he could, but in Anaheim that number was used by Garry Valk, so he opted for 8. In Winnipeg he was able to get 18, and he kept the number with the move to Phoenix, but it wasn't until he joined the Leafs that he was able to get it again. He was attached to the number because that's what his father wore for two years with the Oshawa Generals from 1963 to 1965. Bob Kilger didn't make the NHL, but one of his Oshawa teammates did—a kid by the name of Bobby Orr.

**THANKS TO A LITTLE FLEXIBILITY,** Ken Klee has always had the number he wanted. A stay-at-home defenceman, he preferred the number 2, a solid defensive number that has historically connoted sound and reliable play inside its wearer's own blueline. Klee joined the Washington Capitals midway through the 1994–95 season but was nonetheless given number 2 right away. He kept it for all his eight years with the Capitals, but when he signed with the Leafs for the 2003–04 season there was no way he was going to get number 2—future Hall of Famer Brian Leetch, playing his only season with the Leafs, had seniority and reputation enough to be awarded that number automatically. After consulting with his two children—Garrett, seven, and Mason, six—Klee doubled his favoured digit and went with 22. He had to wear 22 when the Leafs sent him to New Jersey in 2006, was able to get 2 back in Colorado, and was forced back to 22 for 2007–08 when he joined Atlanta, because Garnet Exelby had the single 2. No matter. Klee's affection for two numbers doubled his chances of numeric happiness, and as a result he has never been wanting.

**ALTHOUGH HE PLAYED** only eight NHL games, Vitaly Kolesnik has still had an impressive career. The goalie spent all of his formative years in his hometown in Kazakhstan's Ust-Kamenogorsk region, and attracted significant attention through his play in international events. He played at the 2004 and 2005 World Championships, and it was after the latter that the Colorado Avalanche decided to sign him. That 2005–06 season was a special one for the goalie. Although he spent much of the year in the minors, with Lowell, he appeared in his only NHL games and also played for Kazakhstan at the 2006 Olympics. At season's end, he signed with Mytischi of the Russian league, and he has played there ever since. Whenever he has had the chance, Kolesnik wears number 20 in honour of his hero, the legendary Soviet goalie Vladislav Tretiak. Kolesnik wore this number at the 2005 Worlds and the 2006 Olympics, as well as in his eight NHL games.

**ALTHOUGH ALEXANDER KOROLYUK** hasn't played in the NHL since the 2003–04 season, his career continues to flourish back home in Russia with Vityaz Chekhov, and his name is still associated with the NHL, albeit tenuously. He was drafted by San Jose in 1994 but continued to play in Russia until midway through the 1996–97 season, when he decided to give North America a try. He was assigned to the Sharks' farm team, the Manitoba Moose, but at training camp the following year the speedy forward made the NHL team. He played all of his 296 career NHL games with the Sharks, but these were by no means consecutive. Korolyuk was in the minors part of the time, and at one point he even returned to Russia for a year. He left the NHL for good in 2004, but such is his reputation as a skilled player that he was part of a big-league trade as late as October 2006. The Sharks traded his rights, along with Jim Fahey, to New Jersey for Vladimir Malakhov and a first-round draft choice. For much of his NHL career, Korolyuk wore number 15, but when he returned to San Jose after spending the 2002–03 season with Ak Bars Kazan of the Russian league, he found that Wayne Primeau had been assigned 15 in his absence. So, he switched to 94, in recognition of the year he was drafted into the world's top league.

**THIS IS GOING TO GET CONFUSING,** but it's a story made all the more interesting for that. Tom Kostopoulos was a late draft choice in 1999 by Pittsburgh. He turned pro with Wilkes-Barre/Scranton, the team's American Hockey League affiliate, and made his NHL debut with the Penguins during the 2001–02 season. The Mississauga, Ontario, native has a brother, Chris, who played pro hockey in the 1990s but never made it to the NHL. Chris Kostopoulos, however, is not to be confused with Chris Kotsopoulos, who played for a variety of NHL teams during a ten-year career in the 1980s (note the subtly different spelling—a *t* and an *s* are reversed). Tom Kostopoulos prefers the number 29, because that's the number brother Chris wore, and he was able to secure it when he played with Los Angeles, his home after leaving the Penguins. In 2007, he was signed as a free agent by Montreal, but number 29 hangs from the Bell Centre rafters in honour of Hall of Fame goalie Ken Dryden. Instead, he now wears one of the few single-digit numbers available to a Canadiens player: number 6.

**UWE KRUPP'S FIFTEEN-YEAR CAREER** began with Buffalo in 1986, and throughout his time in the NHL he was almost always able to wear 4. There were only two occasions when he didn't: at the start of his career, when Jim Korn wore 4 for a short time, and during his last year with the Atlanta Thrashers, in 2002–03, when Chris Tamer had 4. In the first instance, Krupp took 40, and in the second case he used 44. "I wore number 4 because my first year in Cologne I was partnered with Udo Kiessling, the best German defenceman of all time. He wore number 4," Krupp explained. "He was my hero and mentor, so when I went to Buffalo, I wore 4 for Udo." Indeed, Krupp was able to keep 4 with the New York Islanders, Quebec/Colorado, and Detroit. Krupp continues: "But, you know, what's interesting is that Udo wore number 4 for Bobby Orr." Furthermore, Krupp's teenage son, Bjorn, now wears number 4 in honour of his dad. So, the connection stretches from Orr to Kiessling to Uwe Krupp to Bjorn Krupp, a span of some forty years and counting!

**EUROPEANS DO NOT SUFFER** from triskaidekaphobia the way North Americans do. That is, they have no superstitious fear of the number 13. A case in point is Pavel Kubina, a longtime wearer of the taboo number. Although he wore number 3 when he first made it to the NHL, with Tampa Bay in 1997–98, he switched to 13 the next year. He wore 13 for the next seven seasons with the Lightning, including 2003–04, when he helped his team win its first Stanley Cup. When the Maple Leafs signed Kubina in the summer of 2006, however, it created a significant dilemma for him, as the incumbent 13 was longtime captain and hero—and another fearless European—Mats Sundin. Kubina decided to go with 73 at first because he thought it looked closest to 13, but he didn't like that number, so he reversed the 1 and 3 to get 31. He's been happily wearing that in Toronto ever since.

**THROUGH CIRCUMSTANCES** beyond his control, Randy Ladouceur went from being a contented number 19 to a contented 29, a number that identified him throughout the rest of a lengthy NHL career. Ladouceur, a reliable yet unspectacular defenceman, was signed as a free agent by Detroit in 1979. After his junior career ended, the Red Wings assigned him to their farm system, and after two and a half years with Kalamazoo and Adirondack he got a chance to play for the NHL team. The rookie wore number 19 in 27 games in 1982–83, but fate intervened that summer: the Wings drafted Steve Yzerman, a superstar in the making who had worn 19 as a junior. Ladouceur, meanwhile, was returned to the minors to spend the early weeks of the 1983–84 schedule. Yzerman claimed the now-vacant 19, and the rest is history: he wore the number for the next twenty-three years, at the end of which the Wings retired it. Upon Ladouceur's return from the minors, he switched to 29, in order to keep a nine in his number. He continued to wear number 29 in more than 900 NHL games with Detroit, Hartford, and Anaheim.

**BY THE TIME GUY LAPOINTE** reached Boston in 1983, his status as a Hall of Famer was certain. The Montreal defenceman had been one of the "Big Three," along with Larry Robinson and Serge Savard, and won seven Stanley Cups in his fourteen years on the Canadiens blueline. Lapointe played with St. Louis in 1981–82 before signing with Boston for his final season in the NHL. Lapointe had occasionally had to settle for other numbers in Montreal and St. Louis before he could get his preferred 5. In Boston, however, the number 5 had more than a little history attached to it. Dit Clapper wore number 5 for the Bruins for almost every one of his twenty years (1927–47) in the league. Of course, when Dit retired, the team retired his number, but in 1966, Clapper suggested to the Bruins that they allow the new rookie, Bobby Orr, to wear it. Bruins management disagreed—this was one of the great numbers, they said, and it would stay retired. When hot rookie defenceman Ray Bourque joined the team in 1979, general manager Harry Sinden asked the Clapper family if the newcomer could wear the number, and they responded with a categorical "no." "We all felt that if Bobby Orr couldn't have had it at Dit's own request, the number should stay retired," Clapper's sister explained. When Sinden signed Lapointe, though, he gave him Clapper's 5 without consulting the family. They were outraged, and public reaction was so strong that Lapointe, who showed poor taste in accepting the number in the first place, switched to 27, the last number of his career.

**A GENERATION AGO,** it was rare to see a hockey player wear a number higher than Tony Esposito's 35, but in this day and age high numbers are commonplace. Just when hockey fans thought they had seen it all, though, along came Guillaume Latendresse of the Montreal Canadiens. Latendresse was drafted by the Canadiens in 2005, and after one more year in junior with Drummondville, he made the Habs at training camp in September 2006. He chose to wear number 84, which turned out to be the last number that had never been used before by an NHL player. Once he played his first game on the opening night of the season, the history books could now report that every number from 0 and 00 all the way up to 99 had been worn by at least one player for at least one game. Latendresse turned out not to be a one-game wonder. He had a fine rookie season and has stayed with the Habs, ensuring that his 84 is more than just a bit of trivia in the history books.

**Brad Lauer**

**OVER A CAREER** that spans some fifteen years and almost as many teams, it would be virtually impossible for a player to stick with the same number. Brad Lauer didn't even try. But his first number, the one he wore with the New York Islanders in 1986–87, will always be special, even though it had no actual significance. He wore number 32 for the first five years, even though he spent a fair bit of that time in the minors. "The trainer in Long Island gave me my number," he explained, "and I had a good training camp, so he said why change it? The organization was also starting to retire a lot of the low numbers so they were getting into the high teens and low twenties, so I took it to a different level. I don't know if it's lucky for me, but I've always stuck to it wherever I've played." Except, that is, for his last year with the Islanders. Lauer started the season in the minors, and by the time he was called up, veteran Steve Thomas had 32, so he arbitrarily chose 10. After that, it was hit and miss, but more often miss. In Chicago, Stephane Matteau had 32; in Ottawa, it was Daniel Berthiaume's number; and by the time Lauer got to Pittsburgh, he didn't care so much. Most often, Lauer was unable to get the number because he was shuffled between the minors and NHL, leaving him low man on the number-choosing totem pole.

**FEW PLAYERS** have made the impact in their first two seasons in the NHL that Evgeni Malkin has made since joining the Pittsburgh Penguins in 2006. He began by scoring a goal in each of his first six NHL games, tying an eighty-year-old record, and went on to win the Calder Trophy for his amazing rookie season, which included 33 goals and 85 points. Playing on an offensive team like Pittsburgh, he is a pleasure to watch. When he plays on a line with Sidney Crosby, as he often does, one is reminded of the good old days in Edmonton when the likes of Wayne Gretzky and Jari Kurri gave opposing goalies headaches. Malkin wanted to take the number 11 when he started with Pittsburgh, but it was spoken for, so he opted for 71 because (like Pavel Kubina) he thought the 7 looked closest to a 1. So, while everyone else sees him wearing 71, he feels like he's wearing 11. Either way, he is one of the league's brightest and most explosive stars. Internationally, he has proven to be flexible with his number. At the 2005 and 2006 World Junior Championships, he wore 17; at the 2006 World Championship, he wore 71; at the 2007 World Championship he wore 11; and, at the 2006 Olympics he had to take 18, because Darius Kasparaitis had 11 and Ilya Kovalchuk had 71.

**ALTHOUGH TORONTO** has been his home since 2000, Bryan McCabe started his NHL career with the New York Islanders five years earlier. He had had a fine junior career in the Western Hockey League, and the Islanders were looking for big things from him right away, both defensively and as an offensive threat. McCabe, however, was slower to develop than the team had hoped, and they traded him to Vancouver. After just a year and a half, he was sent on to Chicago, and only a year later the Leafs got him from the Hawks for nothing more than the oft-injured Alexander Karpovtsev and a fourth-round draft choice. Although McCabe had never scored more than 8 goals in a season before coming to the Leafs, he has since had four seasons with at least 15 goals each, developing into a power-play specialist with a great one-time shot from the point. Throughout his career, McCabe's numeric preference has always been to have a 4 on his sweater. When he started out with the Islanders, he was, simply, number 4. In Vancouver, after a brief time with the uncomfortable 23, he was able to get 4, and with the Hawks he was 44. When he got to Toronto, Cory Cross had 4, so McCabe took 24 for two reasons—first, the aforementioned need to have his lucky 4; and second, because as a kid he always admired Chris Chelios, who wore number 24.

**Dale McCourt**

**IN THE EARLY SUMMER OF 1977,** there was no more prized youngster in the game than Dale McCourt, who was selected first overall by the Detroit Red Wings at that year's Amateur Draft. The twenty-year-old made the team at his first training camp that fall, and he was expected to be the cornerstone of a franchise looking to improve after years of missing the playoffs. He didn't disappoint. In his first four seasons, he averaged about 30 goals and 75 points a year. In the summer of 1978, however, the league ruled that McCourt be sent to Los Angeles as compensation for Detroit's signing of the Kings' Rogie Vachon, who had become a free agent. McCourt caused a stir by challenging the league's system and refusing to go to L.A., and he won. But he was soon traded to Buffalo, after which his productivity suffered, and finally to Toronto. By 1984, his NHL days were done. He ended with 194 goals in his NHL career, a disappointing total considering that he started off like gangbusters.

McCourt was nicknamed Chief because he was part Native Canadian, and his uncle was George Armstrong, longtime captain of the Leafs. McCourt wore number 10 (Armstrong's number) with Detroit, although he couldn't wear the number in either Buffalo or Toronto because it was taken by Craig Ramsay and John Anderson, respectively.

Wouldn't it have been perfect if he wore my 10 in Toronto?

**HAVING PLAYED FOR SIX TEAMS** during his NHL career, goalie Jamie McLennan did plenty of travelling, but the one constant in his life was always number 29, the number he wore because he was a big fan of Montreal goalie Ken Dryden. McLennan wore 29 when he played for his first team, the New York Islanders, starting in 1993, and he was able to keep the number when he left the Islanders to sign with St. Louis in 1996. At his next stop, Minnesota, he wore 29 as well. Then something funny happened. McLennan was traded to Calgary, where he switched to number 33 in deference to popular retired goalie Mike Vernon. There was just one problem with McLennan's noble gesture: Vernon never wore 29! "Out of respect, I didn't wear it [number 29]. Then I realized he wore 30 in his Cup years," McLennan said. When he got to the Rangers, 29 was taken by Boris Mironov, so McLennan kept his accidental 33, but for his next stop, Florida, he returned to Dryden's 29. Oddly enough, McLennan ended his career in 2006–07 back in Calgary, but he made no mistake this time. He finished his career wearing number 29—Dryden's, not Mike Vernon's, number.

**SO FAR,** Derek Meech's NHL career has been reflected by his draft position. The native of Winnipeg, Manitoba, was selected 229th overall in 2002, and he has played only parts of two seasons with the Wings, 2006–07 and 2007–08. He has spent most of his time with Grand Rapids, the team's AHL affiliate. Meech has typically used sweater number 28 there, but in his first call-up with Detroit he was handed number 36 and didn't make a fuss. When he was recalled early in 2007–08, though, Meech asked equipment manager Paul Boyer for a new number, and the two hit on 14, available after the recent departure to the Rangers of Brendan Shanahan. As Meech explained, "Half of 28 is 14, and I used to wear 14 when I was a kid. It's an honour wearing it after a guy like Shanahan." So far, though, it hasn't brought him much luck. Meech played only a handful of games in 2007–08 before being sent back down to wear 28 in Grand Rapids.

**VERY RARE** is the player who plays every game of his NHL career wearing only one number, but then again very rare were the talents of Mark Messier. Only one other player has dressed for more NHL games than Messier: Gordie Howe. Messier is the only player to captain two teams to the Stanley Cup (the Oilers and the Rangers), and in 2007 he was inducted into the Hockey Hall of Fame. Although Messier is known for his number 11, there were brief moments during his career when he had to wear something else. When he played in the WHA, for instance, Messier wore 18 and 27, and when he was demoted to the Central Hockey League in 1979–80 by Oilers head coach Glen Sather for disciplinary reasons, he wore number 10. But for every NHL game he was number 11, because that's the number his father, Doug, wore as a member of the Portland Buckaroos during his playing days. Doug also coached Mark when the lad was a teen playing provincial junior hockey for St. Albert. Given Messier's stature, his claim on number 11 was uncontested—except in Vancouver, where he played three seasons (1997–2000). Number 11 had been unofficially retired for Wayne Maki, and the Maki family was furious that the Canucks didn't consult with them about allowing Messier to wear it. It was the only controversy in a career marked by greatness for Messier.

### DEFENCEMAN
### AARON MILLER

is, if nothing else, one
determined hockey player. Not blessed with all the talent
in the world, the defenceman has nonetheless been in
the league since 1993, a career that began some four
years after he was drafted. The Rangers chose Miller
88th overall in 1989, but the eighteen-year-old was
just starting at the University of Vermont and was
in no rush to make the NHL. After graduating,
he attended the training camp of the Quebec
Nordiques, who had acquired his rights in a
trade with the Rangers. No fabled talent, it was
three more years before he became a regular
with the team, now based in Colorado, although he was called up from the AHL in each
of those three seasons for brief appearances.
Miller later moved on to Los Angeles, and in the
summer of 2007 he signed with Vancouver. The
latter years of his career have been something of
a miracle. Miller missed a year and a half with a
serious back injury, yet his resolve to play again
never left him and he did, indeed, make it back.
Miller, a native of Buffalo, New York, has always

been a huge Babe Ruth fan, and as such wears number 3 whenever he can. It wasn't until the Nordiques (who had retired the number for J.C. Tremblay) moved to Colorado that he finally got this number, and he continued to wear it for his six seasons with the Kings. In Vancouver, though, Ruth's 3 was worn by Kevin Bieksa, so Miller went with the next closest thing, number 4.

**FOR BORIS MIRONOV,** it was always number 2—at any cost. The Muscovite joined the NHL in 1993, with Winnipeg, while his brother Dmitri played in Toronto, and Boris immediately got his favoured number 2 with the Jets. He was traded to Edmonton after a year, though, where Bob Beers wore number 2, so Mironov had to improvise and chose 20. As soon as Beers left, Mironov claimed the 2. Boris was traded to Chicago during the 1998–99 season, however, and it was there that he ran into the first of two serious numeric obstacles. Brad Brown wore 2 for the Hawks, so Mironov had to switch to 3 for a few games. He tried everything he could think of to convince Brown to give him the number, but Brown stubbornly resisted. Mironov, though, believed every player—and every number—had a price, and he proved to be right. In the case of Brown, that price was $5,000, and just like that Mironov was back in a number 2 sweater. The second stumbling block arose when Mironov was sent to the New York Rangers during the 2002–03 season. Brian Leetch was the incumbent 2, and Mironov knew well that the future Hall of Famer would never part ways with the number. Mironov relented and simply chose 29 because it at least had a 2 in it.

**SOMETIMES A LITTLE PATIENCE** and a bit of luck go a long way. Brendan Morrison, a lover of number 7, didn't get his way at first, but he persevered and was ultimately rewarded. "My favourite number was number 7," he explained. "I had that my whole life. Then, I went to play junior hockey [in Penticton] and one of the veteran defencemen had 7, so I went with 17." Things got worse for Morrison when he went to the University of Michigan. Not only was 7 taken (by Ron Sacka), but 17 was also spoken for (by Ryan Sittler). As a result, Morrison went with the traditional number 9, and when he joined the New Jersey Devils to start his NHL career in 1997–98, he stuck with 9. Indeed, he wore 9 throughout his three years with the Devils, until they traded him to Vancouver in March 2000. Happily, 7 was available there, and the British Columbia native claimed it as quickly as possible. He has been with the Canucks, and wearing number 7, ever since.

**Jason Muzzatti**

**IF YOU'RE NOT** the most talented defenceman, you can hone your skills as a defensive defenceman. Not a skilled forward? No problem. You can become a checking forward, a fourth-liner, a superpest. But when a goalie isn't so talented, there isn't too much room for him on the roster. Jason Muzzatti is one such puck stopper, but that didn't signal the end of his career, only a transferring of his skills from the NHL to leagues and countries of lesser calibre. In the NHL, his totals were meagre—62 games played, and a record of 13–25–10. But after some time in the minors, Muzzatti decided to play in Italy, and he has continued to do so for a decade and more. He even played for Italy several times at the World Championship and Olympics, proving that a mediocre player in one league can be a star in another. A Toronto native, Muzzatti grew up worshipping Montreal goalie Ken Dryden, and as such he wears 29 for Italia with near religious conviction. But Muzzatti doesn't stop there. His goalie mask pays homage to Dryden through its design and, in an even more profound tribute, one of his two kids is named...Dryden. Now *that's* devotion.

**THERE MUST BE** a bit of the European in Rick Nash because, as a youngster, he favoured the number 13—not the most popular choice among North American players. Nash has quickly become one of the premier goal scorers in the NHL today. After a rookie season with Columbus in 2002–03 in which he scored 17 times, Nash broke free for 41 goals the next year to win the Maurice Richard Trophy for most goals (tied with Jarome Iginla and Ilya Kovalchuk). But, more recently, Nash is known for two of the most spectacular goals in the modern game. In the final minute of the 2007 gold medal game at the World Championship in Moscow, in which Canada led Finland by a slim 3–2 margin, Nash got the puck near centre ice and stormed in on goal. With one defenceman literally on his back, Nash still managed to deke goalie Kari Lehtonen and tuck the puck home to ensure Canada's gold medal. He was named tournament MVP. Then, in an NHL game in January 2008 against Phoenix, he got the puck at centre, undressed two Coyotes defencemen, deked goalie Mikael Tellqvist, and tucked the puck in the open side. Ever since his family and friends convinced him to drop 13, Nash has worn number 61, and although he won't say why that number is important to him, it seems to have given him his share of luck.

**LONG BEFORE THE NHL** ostracized Ted Nolan as a coach, he was a role player during a pro career that lasted less than a decade. He was drafted by Detroit in 1978, and spent most of his time within the Red Wings' organization. After stints with Kansas City and Adirondack, Nolan made his NHL debut during the 1981–82 season, playing 41 games. His next big-league action wasn't until two years later, and he ended his career in Pittsburgh in 1985–86. Of course, he later became a coach, winning the Jack Adams Award with Buffalo in 1996–97. After rejecting a one-year contract offer from the team, Nolan parted ways with the Sabres and it wasn't until 2006 that he was offered another job, this time with the New York Islanders. As a kid growing up on the Garden River First Nation Reserve near Sault Ste. Marie, Ontario, Nolan was a fan of Bobby Orr and Bobby Hull, and so he wore number 4 or 9 whenever he could. Later, he became so enthralled by the skating of Gilbert Perreault that he switched to number 11. All of Nolan's numeric dreams, however, were fulfilled only in the minors. Because he was a call-up and part-timer in the NHL, he had to settle for the odds and ends that were assigned to him, namely numbers 29 and 8 in Detroit and 25 and 34 with the Penguins.

**BELIEVE IT OR NOT,** Mario Lemieux was not the only NHL player to wear number 66. In fact, he wasn't even the first (though it's a safe bet he'll turn out to be the last). The first 66 was Milan Novy of the former Czechoslovakia. By 1981, Novy was considered a national treasure. He had played for nearly a decade in the Czech league, was named its MVP three times, and led the league in scoring on six occasions. Novy also helped Czechoslovakia win two gold medals at the World Championship, in 1976 and 1977, and he played in the Olympics twice and in two Canada Cup tournaments. Towards the end of his career in Czechoslovakia, the veteran was put on a line with the sensational teenager Jaromir Jagr. Novy left his country in 1981 to try his luck with the Washington Capitals, and he hoped to sport his usual number, 6. But 6 was already spoken for, so he asked the trainer for 66. The trainer, exercising what little power he had over a player's life, refused, giving him 26 instead. In his first game in the NHL, Novy scored a goal and added two assists, after which the same trainer came by and gave him a 66 sweater, realizing this was a star player whom he had to keep happy. The 1981–82 season proved to be Novy's only year in the NHL, and he finished with 18 goals and 48 points in 73 games.

**BEING A TRADITIONALIST,** Wilf Paiement always wanted number 9, the illustrious number worn by the likes of Gordie Howe and Maurice Richard. Indeed, when he began his career with the lowly Kansas City Scouts in 1974–75, number 9 was waiting for him. And when the team moved to Colorado, he was able to keep it. But when the Rockies traded him to the Leafs midway through the 1979–80 season, number 9 was taken. He proposed to do what Wayne Gretzky had done when he encountered a similar logjam as a junior: double the 9 to make 99. Toronto GM Punch Imlach didn't care for the idea at first, and made Paiement wear 14 for his first Leaf game, but ultimately Imlach relented. By the time Paiement was traded to Quebec, Gretzky was so clearly a special player that no one else dared wear his number. Paiement's original number 9 was already taken, by Real Cloutier, so he chose 27. In 1986, the Nordiques traded him to the Rangers, where Dave Gagner wore 9 and Willie Huber had 27, so Paiement went with number 11. In Buffalo, Scott Arniel had 9, so Wilf returned to 27. He ended his career in Pittsburgh in 1987–88, wearing number 9. Paiement's place in hockey history is secure. Because the NHL has retired 99 leaguewide, Paiement will be the last player other than Gretzky to use 99 in the NHL.

**RIGHT WINGER MARK PARRISH** of Bloomington, Minnesota, has been one of the NHL's quietest scorers over the last several seasons. He has bounced around with four teams since 1998, managing to score plenty of goals in whatever situation he finds himself. He has always preferred number 37, even though it hasn't always been available. When he started his career, with Florida, Herberts Vasiljevs had 37, so Parrish went with 21. After being traded to the Islanders, he was hit with a double whammy—Steve Martins had 37 and Mariusz Czerkawski had 21. Parrish merged the two numbers and went with 27, but soon Martins was gone and he could settle into his preferred 37. Parrish managed to keep 37 in Los Angeles, but had to revert to 21 for his current team, the Minnesota Wild. When he played for USA at the 2006 Olympics, however, he was able to wear 37. The number combined two individually important digits for Parrish: his brother, Geno, wore 3 during his minor pro and European career, while his father wore 7 when he played baseball and football. "I'm hoping it'll bring me a bit of luck," Mark said when he first wore 37 with the Islanders.

**Joe Pavelski**

**IN THE OLD DAYS,** a low number was an honour granted only to the stars and veterans of a team, since it meant a lower berth on railway sleeper cars. In the modern era, a low number is still an honour, though the trains have given way to airplanes. Joe Pavelski was a low draft choice by San Jose—205th overall in 2003, to be exact—after which he played two seasons at the University of Wisconsin. In 2006, he went to the Sharks' training camp with high expectations, but although he impressed the management, he was still sent to the minors for additional seasoning. After 16 games with Worcester of the AHL, Pavelski was called up and given the less-than-classic number 53. He played well, though, and showed little sign of trouble adjusting to the faster pace of the NHL. One day, he arrived at his stall in the dressing room to see a number 8 sweater hanging there with his name on it. This was his college number, and it had been put there by coach Ron Wilson as a present to indicate a permanent spot on the team. Indeed, Pavelski stayed up for the rest of the year. He has remained with the Sharks ever since, and continues to wear his low number with pride.

**THERE ARE TWO DIFFERENT** sweater number traditions for Thomas Pock—one for international hockey, and one for the NHL. An undrafted veteran of the Austrian league, Pock was signed as a free agent by the New York Rangers on March 23, 2004. He had played four years at the University of Massachusetts, Amherst, and skated for Austria at the 2002 Olympics in Salt Lake. At age twenty-three, after gaining all this experience, Pock finally attracted the interest of an NHL club. He always wears number 17 for the Austrian national team because that's the number his father wore during his career with Team Austria. But when Thomas got to the Rangers, Chris Simon had 17, so he took what was given him: number 22. The trainer had asked if he wanted 71, but Pock believed the NHL was too classy a league for him to wear a high number, which he felt connoted cockiness and showmanship. And so he has stayed with the Rangers, wearing number 22, ever since.

**PLAYERS OFTEN WEAR NUMBERS** to honour a favourite player, perhaps even their father or a brother. Alexei Ponikarovsky has a different story: he wears 23 to remember the two most important women in his life. The tall Ukrainian winger has played his entire career with the Leafs, starting slowly in 2000–01 and working his way into the roster on a full-time basis by the start of the 2003–04 season. He is blessed with a deadly wrist shot, and over the last three seasons he has averaged 20 goals. He was assigned 39 when the Leafs first called him up, and he later chose 22 because 23, his number since childhood, was taken. He prefers 23 because his mother, Ludmila, was born on June 23, and the number became doubly important later in life because his wife, Inna, was born on November 23. Either way, it's 23 or bust for "Pony."

*Alexei Ponikarovsky*

**FROM 1973 TO 1988,** Denis Potvin played for one team and wore one number. The team was the New York Islanders, and the number was 5. But far from being loaded with significance, 5 was Potvin's distant second choice. During his outstanding junior career with the Ottawa 67's, Potvin always wore number 7, and the team later retired this number in his honour. But when the first-overall draft choice arrived at his first NHL training camp in 1973, he was not a junior sensation, he was a rookie without an ounce of NHL clout. When he walked into the dressing room, he found a number 7 sweater and a note attached to his stall that read: "If you want this sweater, you have to pay me $500. Signed, Germain Gagnon." Potvin ignored the gesture, and instead went for the higest low number available. Ironically, Gagnon, who was no star, was traded to Chicago during the 1973–74 season, but by that time Potvin felt fine in number 5 and kept it the rest of his career.

**THERE IS SOMETHING** of the history buff in Mike Rathje, for he takes his number from an era long before he was even born. A native of Mannville, Alberta, he played junior in Medicine Hat before turning pro with San Jose in 1993. The Sharks had drafted him the previous year, and he quickly developed into a responsible stay-at-home defenceman. He started out wearing number 40, and wasn't able to switch to his preferred 2 until the start of the 2001–02 season. He wore it for three happy seasons before signing with Philadelphia, at which point he had to cede the number to the veteran Derian Hatcher. Rathje nestled in next door with number 3, and he's been there ever since. He started wearing number 2 in junior because he was a huge fan of Doug Harvey, the Hall of Famer who retired in 1969, some five years before Rathje was born.

*Mike Ricci*

**MIKE RICCI** was a perfectly contented number 18 for most of his career. The fourth-overall draft choice in 1990 began his career in Philadelphia at age eighteen, after an outstanding junior career in Peterborough and with Team Canada at the World Junior Championship. He moved on to play for Quebec/Colorado and later San Jose, a reliable 20-goal scorer with a mean streak and a competitive edge few could match. Ricci was famous for his lengthy locks, scraggly appearance, and, of course, toothless mouth, and on a good night he looked like something out of a *Halloween* movie. With Philadelphia and San Jose he wore number 18, but when he joined the Phoenix Coyotes in the summer of 2004 he declared that he was switching to number 40. He wore it to honour Pat Tillman, an NFL football player Ricci had met while playing in San Jose. Tillman, a native of San Jose, rejected a huge contract with the Arizona Cardinals so that he could join his brother in the U.S. Army Rangers in Afghanistan. Tillman was killed in action, the first NFLer to die in combat since the Vietnam War. "When I heard his story, it really touched me," Ricci said. "This is a way to pay tribute to what he's done." Indeed, part of the sales from the Ricci 40 sweaters were donated to the Pat Tillman Foundation.

**Stephane Richer**

**IT'S ONE THING** when a player wears a number in tribute to his childhood hero or his greatest inspiration, but it's quite another when the team anoints him its next superstar and asks him to wear a tribute number of the team's choice. In the case of Stephane Richer, he was drafted 29th overall by Montreal in 1984, not an especially high selection, to be sure. Yet the Canadiens believed he would be the next Jean Beliveau. Richer was called up for a single game in 1984–85 and was given number 22. When he made the team at training camp in 1985, he was given the number 44, a nod to Beliveau's 4 and a clear indication of what the Canadiens expected from him. Despite such pressure, he did indeed excel, scoring 50 goals in 1987–88 and 51 two years later. For several seasons he had 25 goals or more, but the team never went far in the playoffs and Richer was traded to New Jersey. He helped the Devils win their first Cup, in the lockout-shortened 1994–95 season, but soon enough he was on the move again. Richer wore 44 for his whole career except for half of the 1999–2000 season in St. Louis. Defenceman Chris Pronger had the number, so Richer went with 19. His was a fine career that included 421 goals in more than 1,000 games, but the next Beliveau? No, not by a long shot.

BELIVEAU (4)
+ BELIVEAU (4)
= RICHER ? (44)

**Rene Robert**

**TO THIS DAY,** the pre-eminent threesome in the history of the Buffalo Sabres remains the forward unit of Gilbert Perreault, Rick Martin, and Rene Robert. Known as the French Connection Line, these three terrorized enemy goaltenders and led the Sabres on a stunning trip to the Stanley Cup final in 1975, where they lost to Philadelphia in six games. Robert had always worn number 11 in junior hockey but had been given 14 upon breaking into the NHL with Toronto in 1970–71. At least it looked sort of like an 11. He also wore 14 in Pittsburgh in 1971–72, before being traded to Buffalo. There, the number 11 sweater already had an occupant: Perreault, the team's first-ever draft choice in 1970. Buffalo GM Punch Imlach thought 11 was a lucky number, and he had always awarded it to his prize rookies, as far back as his days with the Leafs in the 1960s. Robert stuck with 14, which he was able to wear for the rest of his career, including stints with Colorado and (for a second time) Toronto. When Robert played in the 1973 All-Star Game, Dave Keon wore number 14, so he went with 15. Two years later, Keon wasn't there, so Robert claimed 14.

**Gary Roberts**

**THROUGHOUT HIS DISTINGUISHED** and exceptional career, Gary Roberts has demonstrated a variety of skills. In his early years with Calgary, starting in 1986, the left winger developed a tenacious style that was cut from the same cloth as Gordie Howe. That is, Roberts could score goals as well as anyone on the team, but he could also stand up for his mates. A serious neck injury, though, seemed to end his career midway through the 1995–96 season. Roberts announced his retirement, but over the course of a year and a half decided to, if not revive his playing career, then set himself up physically for the rest of his life. He changed his diet and radically altered his workout regimen, and slowly but surely he felt overall improvement and his neck regained its strength. He signed with Carolina in 1997, mostly because the Hurricanes were the only team willing to risk signing him after such a serious injury. Roberts responded. Although his days of scoring 50 goals were over, he still contributed 20 to 25 goals a season and became famous for his protein shakes and impeccable fitness regimen. With the exception of his time in Toronto, he always wore number 10, in honour of his boyhood hero, Guy Lafleur. "I loved watching him play," Roberts revealed. "He scored a lot of pretty goals playing on the wing with his hair flying in the air."

**MOST FANS REMEMBER** Patrick Roy wearing number 33 with either Montreal or Colorado. The goalie with the oversized equipment won four Stanley Cups during his career (two with the Canadiens, two with the Avalanche) and was named winner of the Conn Smythe Trophy (as outstanding player in the playoffs) three times, in 1986, 1993, and 2001. His rise to stardom was meteoric. In 1984–85, he was with Granby of the Quebec junior league, the league's worst team. By the end of the year he was with Sherbrooke in the American Hockey League, and by the fall of 1985 he was with the Canadiens. The following spring, he earned the nickname "Saint Patrick" for his goaltending heroics in leading the team to an improbable championship, and a star was born. But Roy started the year wearing the unfamiliar number 32. It was only after he established himself as the number one goalie, and the team was able to release colleague Richard Sevigny, that Roy was able to ask for and get number 33, a more symmetrical number, to be sure. He wore 33 for the rest of his career, but anyone with a Patrick Roy rookie card will see him in number 32—it's no misprint!

**BOBBY SANGUINETTI,** who will be coming to the NHL any day now, couldn't believe his luck when the New York Rangers drafted him 21st overall in 2006. An offensively gifted defenceman, Sanguinetti loved watching Brian Leetch play. Leetch, also a defenceman who played like a forward, spent most of two decades in the NHL with the Rangers, wearing number 2. Sanguinetti has followed suit. When he can't get 2, he takes 22, as he did in Owen Sound of the Ontario Hockey League. When he was traded to Brampton, 2 and 22 were taken, so he went with 24. And, when he gets to the Rangers, he will have a similar problem because 2 was retired by the team in Leetch's honour in January 2008, and 22 is used by Thomas Pock. Nonetheless, as Sanguinetti's career moves forward, he will no doubt gravitate towards 2 or 22 whenever he gets a chance.

**ONE OF THE MORE CONSISTENT** and skilled players inside the other team's blueline, Miroslav Satan has been in the NHL for twelve years and counting. During that time he has averaged nearly 30 goals a season and has been a scoring threat wherever he has played. Drafted by Edmonton in 1993, he played first at home in Slovakia and then in the North American minors before making his NHL debut with the Oilers during the 1995–96 season. He was traded to Buffalo after two years, and it was with the Sabres that he really established his reputation. By the time he got to the New York Islanders as a free agent in 2005, scoring goals was what he was famous for. Satan always went for number 18 because his favourite player as a kid was Darius Rusnak, who played in Czechoslovakia. Satan wore 18 in Edmonton (after being assigned number 32 briefly), but when he got to the Sabres Michal Grosek had the number, so he flipped the digits and went with 81. When Grosek left, Satan moved into the more familiar 18, but then he promptly went into a scoring slump and reverted to 81. Furthermore, friends and fans preferred the higher number. "It seemed like nobody liked 18," he said. "Everybody made me feel bad about it, so I had to switch it back to 81." Sure enough, he has been 81 ever since.

**IF MARC SAVARD** isn't the quietest superstar in the NHL, then he is simply the game's most underrated player, a true genius with the puck who has been underappreciated for several years. Drafted just 91st overall by the Rangers in 1995, Savard managed only 10 goals and 51 points in his first two partial seasons with the Blueshirts. Unimpressed, they traded him to Calgary, where he proved to be a late bloomer. Nonetheless, after he played 10 games in 2002–03—his fourth season with the Flames—they sent him to Atlanta, a young team. Given more ice time and more responsibility, and with several years' experience under his belt, Savard became one of the game's premier playmakers. He increased his point totals from 77 to 85 to 97, after which he became an unrestricted free agent and signed with Boston in the summer of 2006. He got the big contract but didn't rest on his laurels, recording 96 points with a non-playoff team his first year and helping the Bruins improve further during the 2007–08 season. Savard always wanted 9, a star's number, but except for his time in Atlanta it was always unavailable. In Boston it was retired for Johnny Bucyk. He wore 71 at first, but quickly changed to 91 since, he says, "It was the closest I could get to 9."

**TWO NUMBERS STAND ABOVE** the others for Teemu Selanne, one of the greatest players ever to come out of Finland. As a rookie in 1992–93 with the Winnipeg Jets, Selanne wore number 13 and set NHL records that might never be broken. He scored 76 goals to lead the league, and finished with 132 points, two benchmarks for a first-year player that seem untouchable. Selanne played for four years in the 'Peg before being traded to Anaheim, where he stayed nearly six seasons. He later played with San Jose and Colorado, and then returned to Anaheim, helping the team to a Stanley Cup win in the spring of 2007. Selanne took 13 in Winnipeg because the number 8 he had worn all his life was being used by veteran defenceman Randy Carlyle. But 13 was fine with Teemu because that was his soccer number. When Carlyle retired, though, Selanne, now a young superstar, took the 8 and continued to wear it for the next decade. When he got to Anaheim in 2005, Sandis Ozolinsh had 8, so Selanne went back to 13. And again, when Ozolinsh moved on, Selanne switched back into the 8.

**James Sheppard**

**IN THE LONG HISTORY** of sweater numbers, there may be no stranger story than that of James Sheppard, a rookie who made his NHL debut with Minnesota during the 2007–08 season. Sheppard was a high draft choice by the Wild, ninth overall in 2006, while he played junior with Cape Breton of the Quebec Major Junior Hockey League. He wore number 15 with the Screaming Eagles and he was able to wear number 15 when he came to the NHL. And why 15? A young man with very big feet, Sheppard wears size 15 shoes!

**Steve Shutt**

**BETWEEN 1973 AND 1977,** Steve Shutt achieved a quirky record by increasing his goal production by multiples of 15 for four straight seasons. He went from 15 goals in 1973–74, to 30, to 45, to 60 in 1976–77, establishing himself as a premier left winger with the Canadiens while they were regularly winning the Stanley Cup. He started wearing number 9 while playing junior hockey with the Toronto Marlboros, but he well knew that that number had long been retired at the Forum in honour of Maurice Richard. After being drafted by the Habs, he discussed the dilemma with trainer Eddie Palchak, and decided to go with number 22, the number he wore for the next fourteen years. Shutt's final NHL stop, though, was the Los Angeles Kings in 1984–85, where number 22 was taken by Tiger Williams. Shutt opted for 11 because it had a similar style, and, as he joked, 11 was "lighter" than 22, something that might help an older player like himself.

**MIKE SILLINGER IS A CURIOUS STUDY,** but not because he has a favourite number and has stuck with it his whole career; in fact, it's just the opposite. For starters, Sillinger holds the dubious record of having played for more teams than any other player in NHL history—twelve in all. Yet, since the 1990–91 season when he started out with Detroit, he has always managed to hold a regular spot in the lineup with one team or another. More incredibly, he has been traded ten times during his career, and in eight of his seventeen seasons he has played for two teams. The list is impressive, and his associated sweater numbers history a mish-mash until the last few years. In Detroit, Sillinger wore 21, 22, and 23 briefly, and then 12 for two years. In Anaheim and Vancouver he had 26, and in Philadelphia 11. In Tampa Bay, he went back to 26, but in his next four stops—Florida, Ottawa, Columbus, and Phoenix—he wore 16. In St. Louis, he moved on to 18, and in Nashville he inverted this to make 81, and for his twelfth and most recent stop, with the Islanders, he went back to 18. That's nine numbers in all.

**Jason Spezza**

**EVERY SERIOUS HOCKEY FAN** knows Jason Spezza wears number 19 with the Ottawa Senators, but for one fleeting moment on the night of June 2, 2007, he wore number 44. During game three of the Stanley Cup finals against Anaheim, Spezza and Sami Pahlsson took coincident minor penalties early in the second period after a pushing and shoving match. Spezza's sweater got ripped during the exchange, and the referees told him he'd have to change. Spezza was given a sweater that came immediately to hand—it happened to be one belonging to number 44, Patrick Eaves, who was a healthy scratch that night in favour of Oleg Saprykin. When his penalty was over, Spezza returned to the ice and played one shift wearing 44. When he returned to the team's bench, the trainer handed him a fresh number 19 sweater, and Spezza was, numerically, back to his old self. Meanwhile, he made history by becoming one of a small group of players to wear two numbers during the same game.

**Eric Staal**

**THE FIRST BROTHER** to come out of the hockey factory known as the Staal family of Thunder Bay, Ontario, Eric started his NHL career in 2003–04 with Carolina. He was soon joined by his brother Jordan, who plays for Pittsburgh, and in 2007–08 a third brother, Marc, lined up on the Rangers blueline for his first season. A fourth and final brother, Jared, is playing junior hockey and will, no doubt, be in the NHL soon. Eric chose a number, 12, that was significant to the Staal family. The patriarch, Henry, had been a pretty good player in his own right in the late 1970s and early 1980s at Lakehead University, although he jokes that he had million-dollar feet and ten-cent hands. He wore number 12 back in his playing days, and that's the reason Eric wears it today. "He's had that number since he was four," said Henry Staal with a chuckle. "He wanted to wear Dad's old number. It's kind of neat." Neat, indeed.

**TORONTO FORWARD MATT STAJAN** wears the number 14 that was worn with such pride and success by Dave Keon, the tiny Leafs captain. Matt's dad, Mike, was a big Keon fan as a kid, and when Mike turned forty, Matt and the family pitched in to buy Mr. Stajan a Leafs sweater with the number 14 on it. To this day, that gift hangs in the family's rec room. But the Keon connection isn't the reason why Matt wears the hallowed number. He does it to pay tribute to his uncle, Rob, who was an outstanding athlete at Father Redmond Secondary School in Etobicoke, in Toronto's west end. He was a fine basketball and hockey player, and always wore number 14, but late in his teens he was diagnosed with cancer. "He ended up dying when he was twenty-two," Matt revealed. "I was only about six at the time. I've worn it [number 14] ever since in honour of my uncle. It just so happens that everywhere I've played, it's been available." Well, not always. When Stajan made his NHL debut with the Leafs, Jonas Hoglund had number 14, so Stajan flipped the digits around and went with 41. He even scored a goal in that first game, wearing 41. Soon enough, though, Hoglund was playing back in Europe and Stajan took the vacated 14.

YOU'D THINK 14 WAS TO HONOUR **ME**, ... BUT YOU'D BE **WRONG**.

**CENTRE PAUL STASTNY** is fast becoming the best American player in the NHL. After a strong rookie season with Colorado in 2006–07, in which he had 28 goals and 78 points, Stastny started 2007–08 so well that he led the scoring race for a brief time. He tapered off a bit but has developed at a pace that pleases the Avalanche brass. Stastny is the younger of two children fathered by the great Peter Stastny. The connection in Paul's case is even stronger because Peter played his best years with the Quebec Nordiques, the team that later became the Avalanche. The Nordiques had retired Peter's 26 in honour of his Hall of Fame career, but the Avs have kept the number in circulation. In 2005–06, the number was worn by John-Michael Liles, but when Paul Stastny came on board, Liles relinquished 26 to Paul and took 4, formerly worn by Rob Blake. Internationally, though, Paul wears number 11 whenever possible because that's the number he wore at the University of Denver. Brother Yan also wore 11 with the University of Notre Dame. In 2007, when Paul played for Team USA at the World Championship, number 26 was used by Erik Cole. Although Paul considered 21 (to combine 26 and 11), he settled on the simple 11.

**THE FIRST OF PETER STASTNY'S SONS** to make it to the NHL, Yan Stastny was drafted a lowly 259th overall by Boston in 2002. While there's no doubt about Yan's hockey lineage, pinning down his nationality can be a bit of a challenge. That's because Peter played internationally for three teams—the former Czechoslovakia, Canada, and Slovakia—and Yan was equally peripatetic. He was born in Quebec City but raised in the U.S. and plays for Team USA when called upon. Both Yan and his more famous brother, Paul, always wanted their dad's number 26, but that wasn't possible, so Yan developed his own identity. "I was always 26 growing up," he explained, "but in my first year of junior I couldn't have it, so I wore 17 for no special reason. Then I had 10. My number now is 11 or 21." In Edmonton, where he made his NHL debut after being traded by the Bruins, he wore the inglorious number 42, and then, when he was traded back to Boston during the 2005–06 season, he took 42 and 43. When he played for the USA at the 2006 World Championship in Latvia, he wore number 22, quite simply because it was assigned to him.

**RIGHT WINGER JACK STODDARD** played in the NHL during the height of the Original Six, squeezing in 80 games with the New York Rangers between 1951 and 1953. Although he was a star scorer in the minors, notably with Providence in the AHL, he didn't produce at the same rate when he got to the NHL and, as a result, his career with the Rangers came to an end. He was unique, though, for wearing number 13 in New York, a number that came to him during his AHL days strictly by chance. "[In 1950], when we got a new shipment of sweaters," he explained at the time, "my old number 20 wasn't among them. There was a 13, however, so I took it. It brought me luck, and I wouldn't want to wear any-thing else now." And he didn't. No one fought him for the reputedly unlucky number, and he happily wore it the rest of his career. He wasn't, however, the first NHLer to sport a 13. That distinction goes to Gizzy Hart of the Detroit Cougars, in 1925–26.

**SMALL, SKILLED, AND SWIFT,** Steve Sullivan is a tiny, perfect offensive package. He had eight 20-goal seasons during a career that started in New Jersey in 1995 and continued to 2007 with Nashville. His was an incredible success story in that he was drafted 233rd overall, so low that New Jersey could not possibly have envisioned a lengthy career for this small player. In fact, the Devils traded him to Toronto in a big deal that saw Doug Gilmour go to New Jersey, but it was in Chicago that Sullivan really started to exceed expectations. In his first full year with the Hawks, 2000–01, he had 34 goals and 75 points. He was later traded to Nashville, but he kept on scoring. It wasn't until he got to the Windy City, though, that he was able to wear number 26, which had always been his first choice. That's because it was the number his cousin, Bob Sullivan, wore in 1982–83 with the Hartford Whalers, his only NHL season. Steve continued to wear it in Nashville, although in Toronto it had been worn by Jamie Heward and in New Jersey by Jason Smith. No matter. Sullivan was happy with the Predators, and they with him, and he wore the 26 with comfort and pride.

**THERE IS A WEALTH** of family inspiration for Jeff Tambellini. His grandfather, Addy, played for Canada at the 1961 World Championship. The country was represented by the Trail Smoke Eaters, and they brought home the gold medal, the last one Canada would win at the Worlds until 1994. Later, Addy's son, Steve, made it to the NHL, where he had a lengthy career, including playing for Canada at the World Junior Championship in 1978. When Jeff played at the World Juniors in 2004, he and Steve became the first father-and-son combo to have played for Canada at the prestigious tournament. Jeff made his NHL debut with Los Angeles in 2005–06, although the Kings traded him later in the season to the Islanders. He wanted number 15 with the Kings, but Jeff Cowan wore it, so he went with 51. On Long Island, the team gave him 51, figuring it was what he wanted, but when he explained that 15 was his dream number, he got it right away. As Jeff explained, 15 was the number that grandfather Addy wore for Canada, and that was reason enough for Jeff.

**THE FIRST INUIT PLAYER** to make it to the NHL, Jordin Tootoo is stocky, strong, and hated around the league as a superpest and agitator. He grew up eating char for meals and hunting using traditional methods, making him, if nothing else, tough as nails. His story was made tragic by the death of brother Terence, who committed suicide before he could make it to the big league. Heartbroken but inspired, Jordin pursued a dream for two, a dream that came true in 2003–04 when he made the Nashville Predators. Tootoo always wore the number 22, of course—"two-two" sounding like Tootoo—but when he first came to the Predators Greg Johnson was wearing it, so he went for 55, which looks like a mirror image of 22. The next time he was with the team, after a year in the minors, Tootoo was able to wear 2-2 to match the sound of his name.

**SMALL BUT FEISTY,** a "shift disturber" *and* an offensive threat, Darcy Tucker is, when at the top of his game, about 180 pounds of dynamite ready to go off at any moment. When he is at his best, his temper is simmering without boiling over, but all too often he loses his cool and fireworks ensue. Tucker started with Montreal back in 1995, but he never made much of an impression and was sent to Tampa Bay as part of a multi-player deal. After playing one full season and parts of two others with the Lightning, he was sent to Toronto, where his career took off as his personality captured the imaginations of Leaf fans. It was in Toronto that he also became an effective player, a finisher on the power play who parks himself next to the goalie's back door and swats home passes sent across the crease. Tucker was always a fan of Bobby Clarke, the feisty captain of the Philadelphia Flyers during the days of the Broad Street Bullies, and as such he always gravitated towards number 16. Of course, that number was retired in Montreal for Henri Richard, but when he got to Tampa Bay it was available. Ditto for Toronto. Tucker has made 16 his own for more than a decade, his style of play and his desire to emulate his childhood hero evident in every shift he takes.

**BY THE TIME HE RETIRED** in 2007, Pierre Turgeon had reached several major milestones and done just about everything a player could want, with one exception: win the Stanley Cup. In a career that comprised 1,294 regular-season games, Turgeon scored 515 goals and accumulated 1,327 points, but over the course of nineteen seasons with six teams he never came particularly close to winning the famous mug of Lord Stanley. He played in four All-Star Games and won the Lady Byng Trophy in 1992–93, the same year he had career bests for goals (58) and points (132), two feats he never came close to replicating. Turgeon always wanted to wear number 7 because of its star quality, but right from the get-go those ambitions were quashed. As a rookie with Buffalo in 1987–88, he saw John Tucker wearing 7 and went with the next best thing. He doubled the number to make 77, and he kept that number for the next 1,200 games and more. The only time he couldn't wear it was during his final two years in Colorado, where it was retired for Ray Bourque, so Turgeon went with 87, the year he was drafted. It was as an 87 that he played his final 79 games in the NHL before calling it quits. He was a player with great stats, but one, perhaps, who lacked that something extra that separates the legendary players from those who are merely very good.

**COMING TO AN NHL RINK SOON** is Kyle Turris, a draft choice of Phoenix in 2007. Selected third overall, in fact, Turris was still in provincial junior hockey when he was chosen by the Wayne Gretzky–coached team. He played for Canada at the eight-game Super Series in September 2007, when Canada crushed Russia by winning seven and tying one. Turris then went on to become one of the heroes for Canada at the 2008 World Junior Championship in Pardubice, Czech Republic, helping the team win its fourth straight gold medal. His contributions were greatest on the night of December 27, 2007, when he scored both goals as Canada defeated Slovakia 2–0. He finished the WJC with 4 goals and 8 points. Turris has always worn number 19, and so far, from junior to Team Canada to the University of Wisconsin where he currently plays, he has been able to keep it. His reasons are simple—he was a huge Steve Yzerman fan when "Stevie Y" was still playing. However, when he gets to Phoenix, he might run into trouble because longtime Coyotes forward and captain Shane Doan wears 19. Turris might have to go for 91, or create a new favourite number for the immediate future if, indeed, it is with the Coyotes that he makes his NHL entrance.

**IN A TWENTY-YEAR NHL CAREER** that took him to the Hockey Hall of Fame, Norm Ullman played for only two teams: Detroit and Toronto. He arrived in both cities immediately after the teams had won several Stanley Cups, but he was fated to play some 1,410 regular-season games without tasting champagne from the great trophy. He also fell just shy of another milestone, retiring in 1977 with 490 NHL goals to his credit, ten short of the hallowed 500 plateau. Nonetheless, Ullman was one of the best players in the game during his day, and he was never shy about wanting an elite number. When he got to Detroit in 1955, after the Red Wings had won three Cups in the previous four years, he was given number 16. He wanted number 7, which he had used throughout junior hockey in Edmonton, but that was taken by another Hall of Famer, the legendary Ted Lindsay. Once Lindsay was traded, Ullman was permitted to take number 7, which the team had not retired because Lindsay had been deemed *persona non grata* for trying to start a players' union. When Ullman was traded to Toronto, he wanted to keep 7, but this time Tim Horton wore it. Ullman selected number 9—another "prestige number," he explained.

**MIKE WALTON** earned the nickname "Shakey" when he played with the Leafs in the mid-1960s because he was so intimidated by dictatorial coach Punch Imlach that his nerves were always on edge. He couldn't have been more relieved and delighted to be traded to Boston, the best team in the league, whose lineup featured Bobby Orr, Phil Esposito, and goalie Gerry Cheevers. Walton was traded to the Bruins during the 1970–71 season, one in which the Bruins were coming off a Stanley Cup win. The Bruins didn't win another Cup that year, but they did win again in the spring of 1972. After one more year, Walton, like so many players of that era, left the NHL to play in the more lucrative World Hockey Association, but after three years with the Minnesota Fighting Saints he signed with the Vancouver Canucks, and ended his career in the NHL four years later. Before he got to Boston, Walton had long been an admirer of Orr's, and the two became very good friends when they were teammates. Indeed, they partnered in the summer to run the highly successful Orr-Walton hockey camp. Walton paid numeric tribute to Orr during his years in Vancouver by wearing number 4, a non-traditional number for a forward, but a great way to show admiration for the man who was arguably the greatest player of all time.

**DOUG WEIGHT AND TONY AMONTE** arrived at the New York Rangers at the same time. Weight had been playing for Lake Superior State University and Amonte at Boston University, but their seasons were over and the Rangers wanted them as insurance during the 1991 playoffs. While both went on to have lengthy NHL careers, at this time they were with the team to learn and soak up the experience as much as anything else. Weight arrived wanting number 11, but that number was taken by Kelly Kisio. The trainers instead offered both players numbers in the thirties. "Tony got 33 and I got 39, and it's been good to me ever since," Weight said. Indeed, he has worn 39 throughout his career— which is now more than 1,100 games strong—with just thirteen exceptions. When he was dealt to Edmonton at the trade deadline in 1992–93, he took number 42 until the end of the year, switching back to 39 for the start of the next season.

## Stephen Weiss

**IT WAS A PRETTY COOL WAY** to begin a career, but in the end Stephen Weiss went with his heart instead of happy circumstance. He made his NHL debut with the Florida Panthers on April 3, 2002, his nineteenth birthday, and the trainer gave him number 19. That night, Weiss went out and scored a goal, so, of course, he wanted to keep the number. But over the summer, the Toronto native realized that number 9 was what he truly wanted, and so to start the next year he made the switch. He has remained with Florida for his whole career to date, and he has kept number 9 as well.

**IT WASN'T UNTIL** early in the 2006–07 season that Duvie Westcott finally got the number 10 he had been looking for since joining the Columbus Blue Jackets some five years earlier. His was a story of determination and ambition, for no team had drafted him when he was eligible. Instead, he attended St. Cloud State University, made a good impression, and signed with the Blue Jackets as a free agent in 2001. He then went to the farm team in Syracuse, where he continued to impress sufficiently that Columbus called him up for parts of the next two seasons. During these two years, the defenceman was given numbers 40 and 42, generic numbers that were at the ready in the team dressing room. When it was clear he would be a regular, he was assigned 15. Once Trevor Letowski signed as a free agent with Carolina, making number 10 available, Westcott requested it and has worn it ever since. Westcott is a native of Winnipeg, and as such was a huge fan of Dale Hawerchuk, one of the Jets' greatest stars, who was a 10 for most of his career.

**BILL WHITE IS THE PERFECT PLAYER** to illustrate
the effects of the 1967 expansion, which doubled the
size of the NHL from six teams to twelve. A hard-working
defenceman, he had played eight years in the minors
without so much as a sniff from any NHL team, but
once the league expanded, he was acquired by Los Angeles
and made the team right away. For the next ten seasons
he played in the NHL with the same effectiveness as in
the AHL, one of dozens of players who had always had
talent but no chance to display it in the NHL. White was
known for his later years with the Chicago Black Hawks,
and even more famous for his participation in the his-
toric Summit Series of 1972. When he joined L.A., he
was given number 21 and didn't complain—he was too
happy just to be in the NHL. But when he got to
Chicago, he wore number 2, in tribute to his childhood
hero, Doug Harvey—whose career stretched from 1947
to 1969, so he was still playing when White made his
NHL debut! Harvey made it into the Hall of Fame, of
course, and although White didn't, his was a career to be
proud of, one that never would have existed years earlier, and one that would have been twice as long had he
come along years later and skated in a further watered-
down league of twenty-one teams and more.

**A 12TH-OVERALL DRAFT CHOICE** by Edmonton in 1991, Tyler Wright turned out to be a significant NHL disappointment, given his excellent play in the WHL with Swift Current. A forward with hands soft enough to score, yet tough enough to fight, he was seen by the Oilers as a power forward of the first order, but when he was called up for several games in 1992–93, he didn't make the adjustment smoothly. He was still only nineteen, though, and the Oilers gave him three more years to work out the kinks—kinks that, as it turned out, had to be dealt with elsewhere. Edmonton traded him to Pittsburgh, and from there he went to Columbus, which is where he had his best years and longest stay. Wright had used numbers 12 and 19 in Edmonton, and 29 with the Penguins, but everything seemed to come into focus for him at about the same time. His arrival in Columbus coincided roughly with the birth of his daughter, Kennady, on May 28, 1999, and, seeking a new start on a new team, Wright chose number 28 for his debut with the Blue Jackets. Indeed, Kennady proved a strong inspiration for him, and he had four and a half good years in Ohio before going to Anaheim for half a season. He kept number 28 there, but by the end of that season, 2005–06, his NHL days were over.

**MIKE YORK,** a native of Waterford, Michigan, looked to an American hero for inspiration. He always admired Pat LaFontaine, a player whose marvellous career ended prematurely because of head injuries, but one who played with skill and class. York began his career with the New York Rangers in 1999, but late in his third season he was acquired by the Edmonton Oilers to help with their late-season push to make the playoffs. He was traded to the Islanders during the 2004–05 lockout, and later wound up in Philadelphia and then Phoenix, his fifth team in just eight years in the NHL. York had to go with number 18 with the Rangers because number 16— the number LaFontaine wore—was being worn by Rob DiMaio. But when he got to the Oilers, York saw that 16 was free and took it. He has been able to wear that number every stop since, with the exception of the latter half of 2006–07, when he joined the Flyers for 34 games. In that part of the world, 16 was sacrosanct because of Bobby Clarke, so York flipped the digits and went with 61. As soon as he got to Phoenix, though, he switched back, wearing the 16 for LaFontaine with pride.

**HE DIDN'T WIN** the Art Ross Trophy in 2007–08, but he came pretty close, and this is a testament not just to the skill of Henrik Zetterberg but to the amazing scouting of the Detroit Red Wings. No player has ever been drafted so low and come so close to leading the league in scoring. In fact, any player drafted 210th overall, as Zetterberg was in 1999, is usually lucky just to get a sneak peek at the NHL. Yet, the 2007–08 season was a breakout year for the Swede. In the previous two seasons he proved he could score (39 goals in 2005–06 and 33 in 2006–07), but this past season he took the team under his wing, so to speak, and catapulted it to the top of the standings. By the two-thirds mark of the season he had already eclipsed his point total of the previous year. Zetterberg has used the unusual number 40 throughout his NHL career—all games with Detroit— and of course a story goes with it. "I wore 20 in junior," he explained, "and when I got to Detroit Luc Robitaille had it so I doubled it to 40." The only time he has gone back to 20 was during the lockout when he played the year in the Swedish Elite League. He dressed for Timra and led that league in scoring, but even internationally with Sweden he returns to number 40. "Forty is my number now," he declares happily.

# Acknowledgements

The author would like to thank several people who have contributed in one way or another to the making of this book. First, as always, to publisher Jordan Fenn for his ongoing support. To editors Jane Warren and Lloyd Davis for making the text, if not sing, then at least warble. To designers Marijke Friesen and Alison Carr for maintaining a high level of presentation consistent with volume one. To Anthony Jenkins for his wonderful imagination and gift of ink. To agent Dean Cooke and associates Suzanne Brandreth and Mary Hu. To Rob Hynes, who partnered volume one and who I hope will be part of volume three at some point. And to the usual gang of family and friends, from Mom to Liz, Ian, Emily, Zachary, and, of course, my wife, Mary Jane, who has never had a sweater number in her life.

*Andrew Podnieks* is the author of more than forty-five books, including *World of Hockey: Celebrating 100 years of the IIHF*; *The Complete Hockey Dictionary*; *Justin Morneau: All-Star Ball Star*; *GEM Hockey*; and *A Day in the Life of the Leafs*. Podnieks has worn number 6 all his life in tribute to Ace Bailey, whose daughter, Joyce, took him to his first Leafs game many years ago. For more information on Andrew Podnieks, please visit his website at www.andrewpodnieks.com.

*Anthony Jenkins* joined *The Globe and Mail* in 1974, where for over three decades he has drawn editorial cartoons, caricatures, and illustrations. During the 1980s, he also began writing for the paper and continues to be a regular contributor. Jenkins has been playing pick-up hockey with the same core group of players (both men and women) for the last twenty-nine seasons. He wears number 50, his age when the sweater was given to him, and the name "Big Skate" (a disparaging reference to his alleged lethargic looping turns) appears on his Brampton Battalion warm-up jersey. He lives in Toronto with his wife and two daughters, and still plays hockey twice a week. For more information, please visit www.jenkinsdraws.com.